The Word

The Word

That Made Us Whole

Cornelius and Christina Browne

To order additional copies of this book, contact:
Xlibris LLC
0-800-056-3182
www.xlibrispublishing.co.uk
Orders@xlibrispublishing.co.uk
300123

Contents

CHAPTER 1

The Word

I T IS THE interaction between the mind and specific scripture verses that will bring about change in the pattern of thought, emotion, behaviour, physical body, and eventually any abnormal condition.

My husband (Toks) and I got married on 5 May 1984. We were Christians on paper but lived like unbelievers. I was not pregnant before marriage, contrary to the prevalent practice in our society at the time (mind you, this was Lagos, Nigeria, in the early 1980s). The belief within our culture was that this would reduce the anxiety of conception for newly-weds, and it was considered unwise to risk not conceiving before one ties the knot. We had made attempts prior to getting married, but it just didn't happen. I guess our long courtship of ten years had created a stronger bond that far outweighed the fear of childlessness.

My mother attended the pre-marriage customary events but died three weeks before our wedding. She had succumbed to over thirty years of chronic asthma and eventually passed away on the day my family formally accepted the proposal from the groom's family. She would have wanted us to carry on with the wedding as planned, and besides, her siblings insisted it went ahead. According to them, not going ahead would bring bad fortune.

The wedding was well attended, and we had a lot of support. My dad and brothers came over from England, where they were based, and my sister-in-law from Miami. We had to take a lot of time off work as a result of the funeral and wedding ceremonies happening in quick succession and had to return to work without having a honeymoon.

The months that followed were very traumatic. We faced a lot of pressure from extended family members who had been eager for news of pregnancy; however, this was not forthcoming.

They were disappointed, and so were we. We were given much advice, and a particular aunt of mine, in her own way of showing concern, confronted us with the suggestion that we did not know what to do, thinking we had not even consummated the marriage.

We eventually sought medical help. After a few investigations, our worst fears became our nightmare. My uterus was found to be retroverted, and I had hormonal imbalance. My husband was told that the state of his spermatozoa was abnormal both in quantity and quality and that he would be unable to father a child. Our situation was hopeless, and we were helpless. The gynaecologist was ready to start us on a course of treatment but said he could not give us any guarantees.

I had regular hormonal injections, and my husband was put on long-term antibiotics. In addition, he was found to have non-specific urethritis, so he also had to take regular broad-spectrum antibiotics. Later, a urologist discovered varicoceles in his scrotum. The high temperature created by the varicoceles was destroying any normal sperm. I taught my husband how to give the injections, and we administered them to each other. He soon became skilled at it.

We went through the motions with no real expectations of success as the doctors never gave us hope. My husband decided that we should try for a child over the next five years, and if nothing happened within that time, we would go our separate ways. It must have been a very hard decision for him to make. This was a very sad thing for me to hear. We had met in our teenage years – he was sixteen and I was fifteen – and we got married at the age of twenty-six.

The pressure grew stronger as we became preoccupied with this unmet need. It was taboo in those days, and you were constantly watched to see if you grew a bump or not. We were introduced to a doctor of divination (traditional medicine man). He used incantations, read horoscopes and sand; he also prescribed potions. He assessed both of us, and his conclusion was that evil people had got involved, but he could fix it. He prescribed potions for us to use and required us to buy pigeons for his divination. He gave us hope of having children but tied us to a condition that we had to return to him for protection for the children because evil people would make attempts to kill them.

Around the same time, my sister introduced us to a Christian couple. This was about eighteen months into our marriage.

To be honest, I cannot remember the whole conversation with this couple, but it went along the lines that God was in the business of giving children. They cited many examples of barren women in the Bible and their deliverance. They gave us hope unlike the gynaecologist. We were invited to a three-day Christian retreat in the countryside. The first miracle was that my husband agreed to attend. This I regarded as a breakthrough because he ordinarily would have turned the invitation down because of his lifestyle.

On the morning of our departure, my husband announced that he was not going to attend the retreat anymore; he had changed his mind. I pleaded with him, suggesting we had nothing to lose by attending; eventually he agreed.

At the camp, we were allocated separate rooms. The women were separated from the men. My husband wanted to leave as soon as we got there, but the men encouraged him to stay. The camp was lively, and the programme was interesting. To us, the people appeared quite strange because they wore a smile all the time; we didn't believe anyone could be that joyful and peaceful. We were engaged in one activity after the other; there was never a dull moment.

The effectual fervent prayer of
a righteous man availeth much.

James 5:16

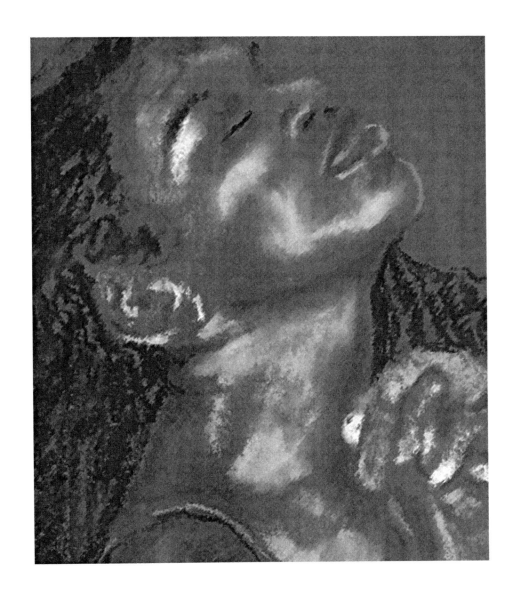

By the afternoon, my sister, who also came along with us, and I were physically exhausted and decided to take a nap. My husband attended the afternoon session, and in this meeting, he had a powerful encounter with God. The message he heard was all about the death of the Lord Jesus Christ. It was delivered in such a way that it was like he had never heard the story of Jesus before. He was arrested by the message and dedicated his life to Christ after that. Hallelujah!

When we met up again later, he told us his experience of how the message of the Cross was delivered and was nothing like he had heard in Sunday school. His eyes were bloodshot, having been deeply moved by this experience. Deep down I was full of joy because I realised he had been touched and he was a changed man.

During the evening programme, we had three well-seasoned Christian men (mature in the Lord) to counsel us and pray with us. Two of them were consultants from the University College Hospital (Ibadan), one a cardiothoracic surgeon and the other a morbid pathologist. They were both very assertive and prayed loudly in a language completely alien to us, but we later learnt that they had been praying in tongues whilst engaged in spiritual warfare.

It was a scary experience, and I whispered to myself, 'God, what is this? Please help!' I was thinking, 'Surely these guys cannot be Christians. They're just fanatical doctors who sound like they are losing it a bit!' However, despite my anxiety, I felt God had sent these three men, for they had ministered to us so beautifully under a special anointing. The Holy Spirit convicted me of my sins, and right there and then I dedicated my life to Christ. That was the beginning of our new Christian life together.

The journey home was pleasant. We were so full of joy it felt like we were floating in mid-air, as if the car tyres were not touching the ground. Our lives had been changed; the translation from the kingdom of darkness to the Kingdom of God was an experience one would never forget.

We never returned to the traditional doctor, and neither did we go back to the gynaecologist. There was no point. One had given us false hope, and the other one gave us no hope. A new door had been opened, and we were both fully persuaded that the hope given to us by the Christians was enough assurance.

A week after our born-again experience, we were visited by the same medical doctors who had ministered to us at the Christian retreat a week earlier. They took us through a couple of scriptures and explained our need for the baptism in the Holy Spirit. After this, they prayed with us to receive the Holy Spirit with the evidence of speaking in tongues. This was a powerful but strange experience. My husband and my sister began praying in the Spirit almost immediately, and for my husband, the encounter was such that he kept being repeatedly lifted off the ground as he spoke in tongues, feeling a surge in his belly.

But I was greatly disappointed as there was no evidence that I had received the baptism in the Holy Spirit. I went to bed in tears, wondering why I was the only one who did not have this wonderful experience. That night I inquired of the Lord why this was the case for me, and by the morning, I woke up speaking in tongues. The three of us spent the morning praising and worshipping God in our new heavenly language. It was truly a beautiful and glorious morning.

He that believeth on me, as the scripture hath said, out of his belly shall
flow rivers of living water.

John 7:38

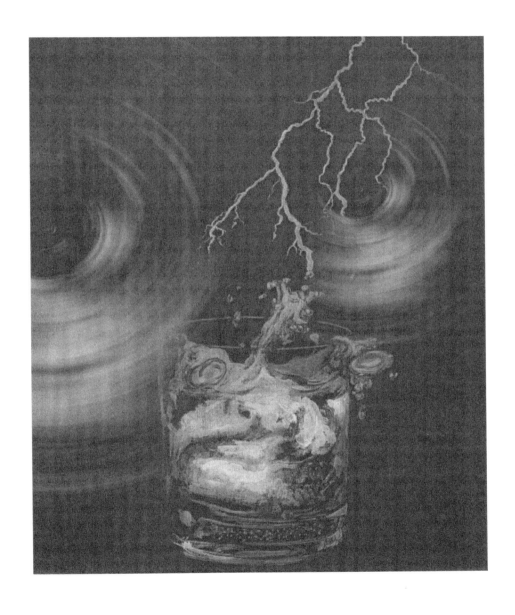

The Vision

Early the next day, I was awakened from my sleep by the sound of my husband praising God at the top of his voice. He had a dream, which he later shared with me. In his dream, he had seen a grey-bearded old man writing a coded message in a book. Supernaturally my husband was able to interpret the code. The message was about his future, which included our first son. The baby was placed in his hands, and my husband was told to name him. He named him Olamide.

At this point, whilst telling his dream, my husband asked me to pick a name for our son. I chose to name him Joshua. I was actually asking God for twins and had given them the names Joshua and Caleb. I later changed Caleb to Jordan.

By faith, my husband would regularly call me Joshua's mum, and I would call him Joshua's dad. Some of our close Christian friends engaged in this name calling as well. Funny enough, my husband also named our daughter Anna-Maria, and this was seven years before she was born (we eventually named her Janet). We called them as if they already existed, and it was fun. Amazingly, it all eventually came to pass.

The Following Years

One year after getting saved, our dream of having children did not materialise. My level of faith began to decrease whilst the pressure from family and close friends increased. We were given all sorts of advice. I became quite depressed, losing my self-esteem and self-confidence.

We had lots of friends who were just starting out as new couples. Naturally, they were having children, and we were expected to attend the traditional naming ceremonies. It was customary in our culture to hold a naming ceremony seven days after a child was born.

We were always late getting to naming ceremonies. It was the embarrassment that was difficult to manage. We felt like complete failures; this was what the culture did to you. The guilt and shame were unbearable.

When people discussed children or pregnancy, a topic which always cropped up in conversations, I would shrink into my seat, wishing the topic would change; but people seemed insensitive, or perhaps it just didn't occur to them that this could be a sore spot for me. I had never fallen pregnant before and envied those that at least had the experience. Even if the pregnancy did not come to fruition, at least that woman could say she was once with child. It was a terrible feeling to have, the thought that one may never bring a child to this world.

One fateful day, I became quite frustrated with the whole business of waiting for the promise of the blessing of the womb. People had given prophecies of how the Lord would answer our prayers, but nothing seemed to be happening, and worse still, it felt that God had become silent on the matter. So I cried unto the Lord, inquiring about the delay we were facing. I was trembling before Him, full of emotion and sweating, when suddenly, as clear as the day, I heard an audible voice. Its strong, powerful sound arrested me and said, 'After your training.' Immediately, having stopped in my tracks, I looked behind me, but there was nobody there except me. When this happened, I had been upstairs alone in my bedroom, and my husband was busy downstairs in the front room.

This was not an auditory hallucination as a result of mental illness; neither was it pseudo hallucination due to sleeplessness or exhaustion. This was the voice of the Almighty.

I wondered what training the Lord was talking about, but I didn't dare ask. This first experience was awesome enough; I did not want an angel to appear to me as well!

Some time went by before I came to understand that 'after your training' meant I needed to get to a particular place in my Christian walk with God before He gave me children. I needed to develop myself spiritually by meditating on His promises. I was made to understand that I could not afford to waste any time. The Holy Spirit still had a lot to teach me, and He constantly ministered to me throughout the training period.

My husband was very supportive; he would suppress his own feelings of frustration to comfort me, particularly during my menstruation, when I would fall into a period of melancholy. Those times, my faith level dipped, and doubts set in. One Christian minister, a very close friend of ours, used to admonish me; he said that if I allowed myself to be discouraged, it was like a regression in my journey of faith. And that was exactly how it felt. The good thing was, after I had my fill of pity party, I made up my mind to get back on track, and that's what I did.

I finally got to that place where my level of faith no longer dwindled, and my menstruation no longer had a negative impact on me because I knew that at His appointed time, God would bless us with children. He always keeps His promise. He has integrity. He is not like man. His will is His Word, and He says He honours His Word above His name. What more did I want?

A lot happened to my husband following the baptism in the Holy Spirit and his encounters with God. God birthed the ministry of gospel art, and this took off in a big way. It involved using pinewood to produce different artefacts and furniture. He later registered a business called Pine Gifts, which flourished for a while in Nigeria.

At the time we got saved, he was an executive art director in a medium-sized advertising agency in Lagos. As a result of the radical change that took place in his life, it was impossible for him to reconcile his Christian ethos with his lifestyle as an advertising director. He inevitably resigned to follow his calling.

The enemy was furious with my husband, and not being well-versed in spiritual warfare, we were dealt large blows here and there. However, we always bounced back whilst at the same time learning how the Kingdom of God worked. It was all part of our training.

After resigning from his job in advertising, he spent four consecutive months at home, where he did nothing but study the Bible intently and prayed without ceasing. The Holy Spirit overwhelmed my husband one morning; he called to me to get pen and paper and asked me to start writing. He read,

The Sovereign LORD has given me a well-instructed tongue, to know the word that sustains the weary. He wakens me morning by morning, wakens my ear to listen like one being instructed. (Isaiah 50:4)

The Holy Spirit gave him clear instructions through these scriptures regarding his first gospel art exhibition in Nigeria as well as ideas on our future ministry, where he would use his skills and I'd use mine.

Following this encounter, my husband fell terribly ill with malaria, and we very quickly realised that this was no match for earthly doctors; we had to call upon the Great Physician. I called some of our Christian brothers, and they prayed powerfully for my husband, and miraculously, he was instantly healed.

His preparations for the up-and-coming exhibition continued. I found these moments to be very precious. I took great pleasure in sitting and watching him as he handled the brush painting so skilfully. For this I loved him all the more; he was incredibly gifted and perfectly made to paint. This was one of the attributes that attracted me to him when we were courting in our teenage years.

Pine Gifts expanded, and he now had a workshop making furniture and building pine kitchens. During one of his business trips, the enemy made another attempt on his life. I was having a nap during this particular afternoon when I was suddenly woken up by the Holy Spirit and instructed to pray. I was drowsy and didn't really know what to pray for or whom to pray for, so I prayed briefly in the Spirit and went back to sleep, only to be aroused again, but this time by a loud knock at the door. It was my husband's friend who, without hesitation, informed me that Toks had been in a road accident, was badly injured, and was now in the hospital. The first thing I asked was if he knocked his chest on the steering wheel, knowing that he would not have been wearing his seat belt. His friend would not tell me how seriously injured he was; everything was left to my imagination.

My gratitude to God our Father is eternal. He woke me up at the right time to pray, and although my prayer was short, it must have made some difference to the severity of the accident. I could hardly recognise him on the hospital bed. He had over twenty stitches on his face, and his hand was badly affected, but there were no injuries to his chest. Thank God. He was in the hospital for ten days. It was the year 1987, September, with just one week to go before his very first gospel art exhibition.

The trials didn't end there. Following the success of his exhibition, my husband was attacked by a pack of ferocious dogs. He had left me in the car to make a delivery to a client who had purchased some paintings at the exhibition. I heard someone shout. As the shouting became more intense, I got out of the car, and to my shock and horror, my husband was being held captive by these dogs biting him all over. Their owner eventually rescued him. He received the appropriate treatment, but this incident was the straw that broke the camel's back, and a few weeks later, we left for Britain.

By this time, we needed to get away, and as it happened, my husband was working on a contract to produce an annual calendar for a commercial bank. He had to have the colour separation processed in the UK. A door had opened, and I seized the opportunity to see my dad and brothers, who were permanently residing in London. After a few days in England, my husband felt strongly that we should not return to Nigeria. We both recognised the great potential for growth professionally if we stayed. So we did. I was really pleased about this decision because on many occasions I had tried to convince him that we should relocate to England. After all, we were both born in England and had the right to live and work there.

So that is exactly what we did; he left me in safe hands and travelled back to Nigeria to take care of business. He sold our belongings, said his goodbyes, and returned to me one month later. The Lord protected him, and we began a new life in London. Four months later, we both started working, he as a senior graphic designer for Newham Council and I as an administrator with the then Department of Health and Social Services whilst preparing for PLAB, an exam taken by foreign medical graduates before they are allowed to practise in the UK.

We joined a vibrant church in North West London. We had just completed their six-week membership class and were starting to settle down in our new spiritual environment when we foolishly left to join another group. The pressure of childlessness convinced us to seek help from this particular group that professed to specialise in helping those looking to God for the blessing of the womb.

At the last service we attended before leaving for this new church, we were called out to the front and prayed for. The Lord had laid our need on the heart of the visiting minister who had called us forward through a 'word of knowledge'. We should have seen that as a red light warning us not to leave the church.

I have stuck unto thy testimonies:
O Lord, put me not to shame.

Psalm 119:31

We left all the same, and the next ten months were a wasted journey; we literally turned the hands of the clock backwards for the completion of our miracle. In this new spiritual arena, we were made to understand that childlessness was a curse and we needed to show an eagerness to be delivered. We were made to fast and pray like there was no tomorrow, but nothing happened. One day after much drama, we decided to leave, and an attempt was made on my husband's life again. He was threatened, but he stood his ground.

In spiritual terms, we forsook the journey to the promised land and took a wrong turn right back to Egypt, but very soon we came back to our senses and returned to our former church, where God had made preparations to receive us back like the prodigal son.

So the faith journey continued. I grew stronger in trusting God. I no longer sank into a depressed mood when I had my menstrual period, and I began to exercise faith by buying things for our children. We already knew them by name, but now they began to acquire belongings. I went out and bought clothes, nappies, safety pins, hats, soft toys (including teddies), and bedtime storybooks to name a few. I had two bags full of them, which I regularly looked through. I would bring the items out one by one and marvel as I looked at them, giggling to myself. I found this to be very therapeutic.

The interesting thing was, at the time, my husband did not show any interest in talking about my bag of baby things, let alone look at the items. However, following a ministration, which I will go into detail later on in my story, he actually asked to have a look. My husband would regularly get a nudge from the Holy Spirit to go back for a medical check-up, but he resisted for fear of receiving bad news. He was worried that the results would have a negative impact on his faith and possibly on his Christian walk.

The pressure once again started mounting from overseas, and we were forced to make a decision and visit a specialist. So off we went to Harley Street. The first thing my husband was asked to do was to take a fertility test. He had semen analysis and was also referred to a urologist because of his history of scrotal varicocele. As for me, I was now diagnosed with endometriosis and referred for surgical exploration of my reproductive organs. I didn't like the sound of it and became distraught. The semen analysis showed a very disappointing result. The sperm count was worse than the results five years previously. His fears were confirmed, and we were back to square one – at least this is what we thought. Returning home numb, I broke down in tears about having to have an exploration done. But as always, my husband comforted me and assured me that I did not have to go through any surgical intervention if I didn't want to, particularly as I expressed no hope in such a procedure but the potential for further complications.

Although my husband received a bad result from the semen analysis, the urologist could not find any varicocele. The reason was that my husband had undergone supernatural surgery in a dream a couple of months before where the varicose veins were removed. He hopes to write a book on his supernatural encounters at a future date. Suffice it to say, God graciously gave my husband a gift of faith when we returned home, and the events that followed were exciting.

He said he was certain the results from the sperm analysis were not his. We had a friend, a Christian sister, staying with us who had just arrived from Nigeria. We shared the problem with her. My husband requested that she lay hands on him and pray because he was certain God would perform a miracle. Right now, as I am writing this, everything seems so surreal, but that is exactly what happened.

Toks went back to the urologist for another test. At the clinic he was told that he needed to wait three months for new sperm to be produced and that doing a test so soon after the previous one would simply produce the same results. But my husband insisted on having the test immediately. The urologist obliged.

When he went to collect the new result, the first question the doctor asked was, 'Where did you do the first test?'

'Here,' my husband replied.

The urologist then said, 'This is embarrassing.'

Your guess is as good as mine! Yes, the result was dramatic; his sperm count had gone from hopeless to positive. The motility rate had also improved.

As we approached our miracle, the support from our Christian friends escalated. Although we had regular support throughout 1990, this time it was different. I remember one particular gathering in our home. We were asked to kneel down. Then prayers were said, and words of knowledge were given. It was like chains were broken, and the atmosphere was spiritually and emotionally charged.

The leader of our local cell group was so convinced after that ministration that I would conceive, and he would constantly ask me if I was with child. The fellowship through which we had become Christians in Nigeria, the Advertisers of Jesus Christ, had supported so many couples that were infertile, and they did not doubt that we would have children. I regularly fasted and prayed with a friend of mine, a gynaecologist. We would break our fast and pray together over the telephone; distance was not a barrier.

Towards the end of 1990, Norvel Hayes, the reputable American evangelist, came to visit our local church. He held a week-long workshop on the importance of worship. He said this was the source of his success and prosperity.

One evening, he invited all the women believing God for children to come to the front, stand next to one another, hold out our arms as if we were carrying our babies, and praise God. We all did as he said, and he gave a word of knowledge on how a lot of us would return the following year to give glory to God. That was the night my husband asked me to bring the bags full of baby things I had collected over the months. I got so excited. As he picked each piece of clothing, he said he could actually visualise the children wearing them in his mind's eye. Praise God.

I engaged in praising God regularly, thanking Him for making me a joyful mother of children. On 9 November 1990, I had my last menstrual period for a long time to come, and that date became the date the midwife used in calculating my EDD (expected date of delivery). This is my husband and my father's birthday, so don't tell me God doesn't have a sense of humour! For the ten days that I did not have my period, I suspected something significant had happened, but I did not utter a word about it to my husband or anyone else. I kept it all to myself and told myself, 'If God can keep the baby for one day and then ten days, He can keep the baby for the duration of the pregnancy.' That assumption strengthened my faith.

Joy Christian Fellowship, our cell group, held a Jesus March in Tottenham at this time, and whilst we were busy preparing, our leader kept asking me if anything had happened. I participated in the march and attended the outreach meeting we had organised to round up the march.

At the meeting, the visiting minister called out women who wanted children. This time I did not go to the front. My husband was shocked; he eyed me and said I should go forward. I tried to tell him that I had missed my period for ten days, but it did not register. He encouraged me to go forward, so I did. When the minister saw me, immediately he said God was going to give me three children. At that point, I knew without a shadow of a doubt that the Lord had come through for us and that I was indeed with child. I had not as much done a pregnancy test, but I believed.

The cell group leader called during the very early hours of one morning and asked me again if I had done the pregnancy test. He knew by the Spirit that God had answered our prayers following the powerful ministration we'd received a couple of months before, and he knew it was only a matter of time. I could no longer call his bluff. My husband and I decided I needed to have a pregnancy test done. I did have one done, and the pregnancy was officially confirmed. Praise God.

Usually when a Christian experiences a breakthrough, it winds the enemy up, and retaliation occurs. This major breakthrough of ours attracted some attacks, but by this time, the enemy was fighting a fortified city. There were threats of miscarrying, but we stood firmly on God's promise. His precious armour was our shield, and we were fighting the good fight.

If we confess our sins, he is faithful and just to forgive us our sins, and to cleanse us from all unrighteousness.

1 John 1:9

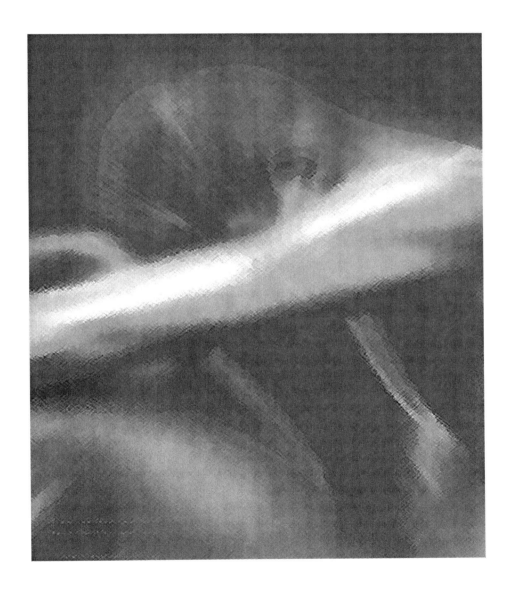

CHAPTER 2

The Prescription

WHEN YOUR DOCTOR writes you a prescription for medicine, you are advised to take it as instructed. You may be warned that if you do not follow instructions, the prescribed medication will not be effective; if taken excessively, it can cause adverse reactions; or it may interact with other medications, leading to side effects.

I will always remember one particular letter sent to me by my niece's nan in Nigeria. In the letter she advised me to read particular scriptures three times a day, as if I were taking prescription medicine. This would eventually prove very fruitful.

Faith does not fear facts. (Michael Bassett)

The gynaecologist we saw left us with no hope; as far as his scientific knowledge would allow, he was just giving us facts based on his medical understanding. Infertility stared us both in the face, and naturally speaking, there was nothing we could do about it.

The gynaecologist said he would try and treat us but gave us no guarantees. But thanks be to God, the Bible says, 'He sent His Word and it healed us.' The Word of God was to be our prescription, and all our hope was placed on it. We took it in a variety of digestible quantities – in the form of prayer and praise, drama, art, and meditating scriptures to name a few. Unknown to us at that time, the different Christian activities we engaged in were helping to administer the Word to our physical bodies, very much like the various forms of medication a doctor would prescribe, such as a capsule, a tablet, a liquid, an injection, or intravenously. These different forms have various properties that will ensure the medicine gets to the right place, having maximum impact. We now have an individualised approach when we prescribe the Word of God as medicine. Meditating on the Word is paramount, whether through engaging in art workshops, singing, drama, or just pondering on scriptures from the Bible.

Meditation

My husband and I had a number of scriptures that we would meditate on. Isaiah 54:1 featured very prominently. One day a Christian friend named Bola, who came to visit, sat on my bed and told me the story of how she had been barren too and was given this very same scripture to meditate on. And she assured me that it would work. God is no respecter of persons, and if He did it for me, He will do it for you too.

> Sing, O barren, thou that didst not bear; break forth into singing, and cry aloud, thou that didst not travail with child: for more are the children of the desolate than the children of the married wife, saith the LORD.

> Enlarge the place of thy tent, and let them stretch forth the curtains of thine habitations: spare not, lengthen thy cords, and strengthen thy stakes;

> For thou shalt break forth on the right hand and on the left; and
> thy seed shall inherit the Gentiles, and make the desolate cities
> to be inhabited. (Isaiah 54:1-3)

This scripture helped me develop a sense of preparedness. It raised my expectation, and my faith level increased.

The Bible is filled with so many promises that will keep you going at every point of your journey. All you need to do is search the scriptures with the guidance of the Holy Spirit.

> So then faith cometh by hearing, and hearing by the word of
> God. (Romans 10:17)

> For thou shalt eat the labour of thine hands: happy shalt thou
> be, and it shall be well with thee.

> Thy wife shall be as a fruitful vine by the sides of thine house:
> thy children like olive plants round about thy table.

> Behold, that thus shall the man be blessed that feareth the
> LORD. (Psalm 128:2-4)

'Thy wife shall be as a fruitful vine by the sides of thine house: your children like olive plants round about thy table.' My husband owned this; he made regular confessions of this, and I confessed it for myself too. And till today, by the special grace of God, I continue to be what he confessed me to be.

I am a fruitful vine by the side of his house; our children are like olive plants round about his table. Children are a reward from God. He wants us to have children, and He needs us to have children. He wants godly offspring.

Sing, O barren, thou that didst not
bear; break forth into singing,
and cry aloud, thou that didst not
travail with child: for more
are the children of the desolate
than the children of the married
wife, saith the LORD.

Isaiah 54:1

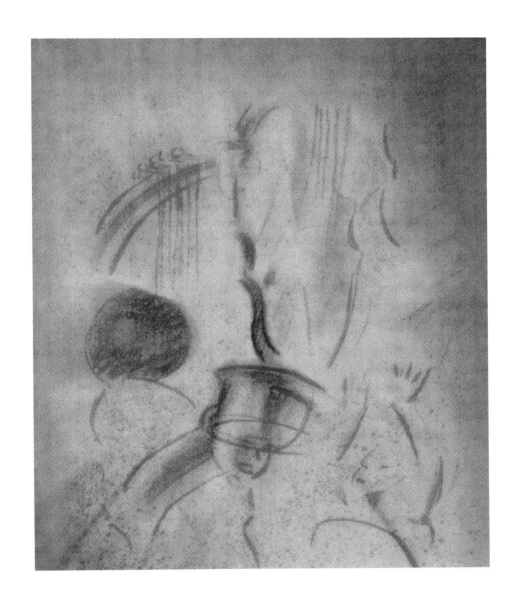

Lo, children are an heritage of the LORD: and the fruit of the womb is his reward.

As arrows are in the hand of a mighty man; so are children of the youth.

Happy is the man that hath his quiver full of them: they shall not be ashamed, but they shall speak with the enemies in the gate. (Psalm 127:3-5)

And did not he make one? Yet had he the residue of the spirit. And wherefore one? That he might seek a godly seed. Therefore take heed to your spirit, and let none deal treacherously against the wife of his youth. (Malachi 2:15)

From time to time, whenever I was a bit discouraged for whatever reason, God would give me another prescription, such as Jeremiah 29. I was not to stop living because I did not have children. I needed to fulfil my dreams in other areas of my life, trusting that God was working on my behalf and that He will never be late but always be on time.

Thus says the Lord of Hosts, the God of Israel, to all who were carried away captive, whom I have caused to be carried away from Jerusalem to Babylon: Build houses and dwell in them; plant gardens and eat their fruit. Take wives and beget sons and daughters to husbands, so that they may bear sons and daughters – that you may be increased there, and not diminished . . . .

For thus saith the lord, that after seventy years be accomplished at Babylon I will visit you, and perform my good word toward you, in causing you to return to this place.

For I know the thoughts that I think toward you, saith the Lord, thoughts of peace and not of evil, to give you an expected end. (Jeremiah 29:4-6, 10-11)

Forty years old was I when Moses the servant of the Lord sent me from Kadeshbarnea to spy out the land; and I brought him word again as it was in mine heart. Nevertheless my brethren that went up with me made the heart of the people melt: but I wholly followed the Lord my God. And Moses swore on that day, saying, surely the land whereon thy feet have trodden shall be thine inheritance, and thy children's forever, because thou hast wholly followed the Lord my God. And now, behold, the Lord hath kept me alive, as He said, these forty and five years, even since the Lord spake this word unto Moses, while the children of Israel wandered in the wilderness: and now, lo, I am this day fourscore and five years old. And as yet I am as strong this day as I was in the day that Moses sent me: as my strength was then, even so is my strength now, for war, both to go out, and to come in. (Joshua 14:7-11)

Caleb was eighty-five years old when he finally got the promise he was given forty years before. He testified that, at eighty-five years of age, he was as strong as he was at forty, when he was given the promise. Moreover, he did not need to fight for it; it was given into his hands. Those very scriptures were what I needed to put me back on track. So I faced my career, did more exams, and started to specialise in the field of psychiatry. I had the impression that this was connected to the good work God had called me to do. Every one of us is being called to do good work.

For we are His workmanship, created in Christ Jesus unto good works, which God hath before ordained that we should walk in them. (Ephesians 2:10)

I knew God had called me to minister and that the ministry was a service to the mentally unwell. Throughout my training, the Lord put Christians with mental health problems along my path, and this further encouraged me that I was treading the right path. He led me to minister to the right people and blocked any attempt to minister where He had not led me. I think this protected me from getting into trouble with the establishments as speaking about the Christian faith was forbidden in my time; you could be dismissed if you were not careful. It was when I did my master's and took on psychiatry and religion as a topic for my dissertation that I realised the battle ahead of me, but the Lord was always there to protect me.

Norvel Hayes, an American minister, once said in a meeting we attended how praising God every day had a tremendous effect on his life. Hearing this made a big change to our walk with God. Andrew Wommack also said that 'praise has an effect on us, God and the devil'. God inhabits the praises of His children.

So another prescription given me was in the form of Psalm 113:9.

He maketh the barren woman to keep house.

He already calls you a mother for it is God that calls those things that be not as though they were (Romans 4:17).

We have to walk by faith just as the scriptures encourage us to do.

Even so faith, if it hath not works, is dead, being alone. (James 2:17)

Was not Abraham our father justified by works, when he had offered Isaac his son upon the altar?

Seest thou how faith wrought with his works, and by works was faith made perfect? (James 2:21-22)

The bible tells us that faith pleases God.

> But without faith it is impossible to please Him: for he that cometh to God must believe that He is, and that He is a rewarder of them that diligently seek Him. (Hebrews 11:6 KJV)

When we exercise faith, we honour God. We show that we trust Him. We are called the just, and as such, we ought to live by faith.

> But the just shall live by faith. (Habakkuk 2:4)

I read Psalm 113:9 every morning, using it to praise God as it says. And within a couple of months, I conceived.

We are never to become so discouraged that we stop believing; like David, we must encourage ourselves (1 Samuel 30:6). We have all the resources to do that in the scriptures. Spend some time praising God. Let the praises flow from your heart and see the result even in the way you feel.

> Cast not away therefore your confidence, which hath great recompense of reward. For ye have need of patience, that, after ye have done the will of God, ye might receive the promise. (Hebrews 10:35-36)

Jeremiah said he took the Word and ate them (Jeremiah 15:16).

> What you eat becomes one with you. (Phil Jackson, a chemistry tutor and pastor)

If you want the perfect medicine, then take the Word of God. You have nothing to lose but so much to gain.

Even science agrees with the Word of God. When you think the right thoughts, they repair the brain, but wrong thoughts cause stress to our brain, sending harmful messages to our cells, and our bodies can eventually become diseased.

As a man thinks, so is he.

> For as he thinketh in his heart, so is he. (Proverbs 23:7)

The Bible also tells us that it is our spirit that sustains us in sickness (Proverbs 18:14). The spirit needs to be in communication with God through His Word. He is a Spirit, and we have a spirit. Meditating on His Word will keep us in tune with God.

God said, 'Draw near to me, and I will draw near to you.' Can you see how we are already receiving from God?

Practical Application

The scriptures have embedded in them sophisticated tools that can initiate dramatic physiological, psychological, biological, chemical, and spiritual recovery.

Follow the instructions according to Proverbs 4:20-21, and your joy will be full.

As Christians we have so many resources within us. All we need is a booster dose of spiritual medicine likened to a booster dose of tetanus vaccine to fortify our immune system when we sustain a contaminated wound.

Give unto the Lord the glory due unto his name: bring an offering, and come before him: worship the Lord in the beauty of holiness.

1Chronicles 16:29

CHAPTER 3

How to Overcome

And they overcame him by the blood of the Lamb, and by the word of their testimony; and they loved not their lives unto death. (Revelations 12:11)

REMEMBERING WHAT THE Lord has done in our lives and in the lives of others is a very powerful tool to receiving His promise. So does reading powerful testimonies in the Word of God.

It has the ability to generate the same emotions it did when the event happened, and it helps to keep good memories alive in us, and this is healthy. So as you listen to the testimonies of other people, you also build up a good memory, and this is what we want – to lay good memories on the bad ones.

As we read or listen to testimonies that directly relate to our situation, we build our faith also. We cannot afford to take our eyes off the promise because the enemy will always try to bring things our way to discourage us. But we must know that whatever we see today is subject to change.

Things seen are temporal; things not seen are eternal. And this is the truth (see 2 Corinthians 4:18).

It is a matter of time, and we need to learn the art of patience. James tells us to count it all joy when we fall into diverse temptation, because when our faith is tested, the product is patience, and patience needs to be allowed to have its perfect work (James 1:2-4). Our waiting time has a purpose. God will never waste time.

The Bible says not one jot of His Word will go unfulfilled.

> For as the rain cometh down, and the snow from heaven, and returneth not thither, but watereth the earth, and maketh it bring forth and bud, that it may give seed to the sower, and bread to the eater: so shall my word be that goeth forth out of my mouth: it shall not return unto me void, but it shall accomplish that which I please, and it shall prosper in the thing whereto I sent it. (Isaiah 55:10-11)

There were moments when unbelief wanted to creep in, so I had to start studying the Word again. I needed to get back up there in my faith level, and as a result, I started to grow and develop in faith again. Take steps of faith towards the promise. That will make the enemy mad, but he will realise that you mean business. I did just that; I bought baby clothes and toys of all sorts. Remember, faith without works is dead.

My husband had his fair share of unbelief. He refused to enjoy the moments I had set aside to look through the baby things, until the day we returned from a Norvel Hayes ministration at our church then, Victory Christian Centre.

> The law of the Lord is perfect, converting the soul; the testimony of the Lord is sure, making wise simple. (Psalm 19:7)

Immediately after we got home, he asked to see the two bags full of baby products. He told me, as he picked up each little item of clothing, that he could actually visualise our baby in it. He was seeing our firstborn, Joshua. I suppose the feeling was reinforced by the dream he'd had some years ago, where God put in his hand a boy child and told him to give the baby a name. He named him Olamide, and I called him Joshua.

God made Abraham the father of many nations when he did not have a child, and more so had gone on in age. God is the one that calls those things that be not, as though they exist.

We have to demonstrate our faith by taking steps that show we believe. Abraham was asked by God to look up at the stars – his family was going to be uncountable – and he also was asked to look at the grains of sand (Genesis 15:5; Hebrews 11:12).

God helped his imagination, which eventually helped his faith to develop and grow. Abraham hoped against hope 'that he might become the father of many nations, according to that which was spoken, so shall thy seed be' (Romans 4:18).

He believed that He who had promised was capable of delivering. He is God Almighty, the 'I am that I am'. The one that never lies.

> That by two immutable things, in which it is was impossible for God to lie, we might have a strong consolation, who have fled for refuge to lay hold upon the hope set before us: which hope we have as an anchor of the soul, both sure and steadfast, and which entereth into that within the veil. (Hebrews 6:18-19)

One thing that will stop you from receiving your healing from God is unbelief, whereas faith as small as a mustard seed will get you your healing. But how does that work?

> The same Spirit that raised Christ from the dead dwells in our mortal body and it can quicken our mortal body to receive healing. (Romans 8:11)

This is what happened to Sarah's body:

> Through faith also Sarah herself received strength to conceive seed, and was delivered of a child when she was past age, because she judged Him faithful who had promised. (Hebrews 11:11)

Sometimes unbelief is present to a certain degree even when you have faith. You need to check yourself. Unbelief creeps in when people pass negative comments or are not in agreement with you.

> He staggered not at the promise of God through unbelief; but was strong in faith, giving glory to God; and being fully persuaded that, what He had promised, He was able also to perform. (Romans 4:20-21)

I was once given a book written by a Christian suggesting adoption as an option. But adoption was not an option for me personally. I had made a choice to trust God and wait for my time of blessing. So I binned the book because it was capable of introducing some unbelief. I needed to stand on the promise of God at all cost (Ephesians 6:13). Jesus could not do much work there because of unbelief (Matthew 13:58).

Share your desires with people who will agree with you; otherwise, you run the risk of reconsidering where you stand in your faith building (Matthew 18:19). Having done all, stand!

The Bible tells us that when two of us agree, whatever we agreed on shall surely come to pass. Do you and your partner agree? My husband and I had a bit of problem in that area. Let him tell you how that came about.

CHAPTER 4

My Husband's Comments

FEAR TRIGGERS 1,400 toxic chemicals in the body. Scientists tell us these chemicals are capable of rendering a person temporarily immobile, confused, drained, and doubting. I put going back to seeking medical help at the back of my mind. This is not a wise decision, as it did not help our corporate faith. I refused to look at the baby products my wife had collected because of unbelief.

'There was no pregnancy, why should I look at baby things?' I thought.

But Jesus said blessed are those who believe without seeing. I had a bit of Thomas mentality in me, but thank God, I soon repented.

Practical Application

Make sure you seek medical advice. It is important you find out what is going on medically. That is sensible.

Always pray that God will give the doctors the understanding and wisdom to deal with your case. In doing this you have already honoured God and acknowledged Him as the person to solve your problem. In our case we did seek medical advice, and we were told they did not have any answers to our problem but they were willing to try various options. They made it easy for us to totally rely on God.

Jesus said, 'If you abide in me and my Words abide in you, you will ask what you will and it shall be done unto you' (John 15:7).

> Meditate upon these things; give thyself wholly to them; that thy profiting may appear to all. (1 Timothy 4:15)

Meditate upon these things; give
thyself wholly to them; that
thy profiting may appear to all.

1 Timothy 4:15

CHAPTER 5

Talk about Drama

THE ENEMY ALWAYS likes to create a scene, particularly when he can't have his way. He also likes to build a mountain out of a molehill. But what we know for definite is that he is already a defeated foe and we are the victors. Amen! Because we do not always know this, he sneaks in quietly.

> Be sober, be vigilant; because your adversary the devil, as a roaring lion, walketh about, seeking whom he may devour. (1 Peter 5:8)

So the apostle Paul advises us to be vigilant. However, we must not fear unduly because Jesus assured us in the scriptures to be of good cheer because He has overcome the world.

My LMP (last menstrual period) was on 9 November, so did this mean no more periods for the next nine months? I missed my period, and that was a revelation because I never miss my periods. Day one passed, day two, day three.

> For there is no restraint to the Lord to save by many or by few.
> (1 Samuel 14:6)

I never told a soul, not even my husband. This was a very crucial time. If the enemy got wind of this, he would begin to play games with my mind, bringing the spirit of doubt. The enemy is always trying to play mind games with us, and we need to be aware of his strategies at all times. He must not be allowed to get one over us. He has been around for a very long time and has met quite a number of human beings – some like you, some like me. And he studies people, both their weaknesses and strengths. Therefore, we too have to be smart and keep in tune with the Lord all the time.

> For to be carnally minded is death; but to be spiritually minded
> is life and peace. (Romans 8:6)

I could not afford for the enemy to play mind games with me, so I said to myself, 'If God can keep this conception for one day, He can keep it throughout the gestation period until delivery.' I had made up my mind that this was what I'd choose to believe, so no matter what happened I was going keep to this belief. This was very powerful, as you will soon find out.

Avoid any opportunity for anxiety. Isaiah 26:3 says, 'Thou wilt keep him in perfect peace, whose mind is stayed on thee: because he trusteth in thee.' He will keep in perfect peace he whose imagination is stayed upon Him. Philippians 4:6-7 also says, 'Be careful for nothing; but in every thing by prayer and supplication with thanksgiving let your request be made known unto God. And the peace of God, which passeth all understanding, shall keep your hearts and minds through Christ Jesus.'

I was not to be anxious for anything, and I was determined not to be anxious. We had come this far, and we had to go all the way. However, six weeks into gestation, I started bleeding. This was a crucial time to get the confession going – I mean speaking the scriptures into your situation.

> Being confident of this very thing, that He which hath begun a
> good work in you will perform it until the day of Jesus Christ.
> (Philippians 1:6)

Again He said in 1 Samuel 3:12, 'In that day I will perform against Eli all things which I have spoken concerning his house: when I begin, I will also make an end.'

I went to the hospital and was put on bed rest. The bleeding continued almost throughout the pregnancy, but we never stopped confessing the Word. There is tremendous power available to us when we confess the Word. Never forget the properties of the Word of God.

It is powerful, living, and sharper than any two-edged sword (Hebrews 4:12). God likened it to fire and a hammer (Jeremiah 23:29). It washes clean, it converts the soul, it never fails, it heals, and so on and so forth. The function and benefits never end.

At four months, I went to the hospital following a bleed. The nurse could not detect a heartbeat, and they told me the baby was probably dead. Well, that was not the Lord's report (Isaiah 53:1).

What is the Lord's report? We need to always challenge words that do not line up with God's Word because God always has the last word (Isaiah 55:11).

My husband enlisted the help of some Christian friends to pray for us. And the next day, when scanned, the baby was happy, and he was somersaulting to the surprise of the nurses.

I had a planned caesarean section at thirty-seven weeks to avoid any complications, as suggested by the consultant. The interesting thing is, the devil cannot just fold his hands and sit back. He always wants to have a piece of the action, but don't let him! Stick to the promise. God will never fail. Doubt your doubts and believe God every time.

There were also dramas with our other two children, but God always had the final word. The enemy does not fight if there isn't anything worth fighting for. Remember how he got wind of the Messiah being born. One of his agents (King Herod) ordered that all male babies be killed, hoping that the Messiah would be one of them. He is actually not as knowledgeable as people think. God has put a limit on him. Only God knows what is in your heart, and the devil gets to know it when you inform him.

> The spirit of a man is the candle of the Lord, searching all the inward parts of the belly. (Proverbs 20:27)

> For what man knoweth the things of a man save the spirit of man which is in him? Even so the things of God knoweth no man, but the Spirit of God. (1 Corinthians 2:11)

Solomon said in the Book of Ecclesiastes that there is nothing new under the sun and no one should be surprised about the evil machinations of Satan; he does not have any new tricks. Drama is what he does, but we have the mind of Christ and can discern his devices. What's more, we have weapons of warfare, and our success is guaranteed all the time. Whether we live or die, we win every time. Praise God!

Practical Application

Dig your heels in. Refuse to do what the enemy is suggesting. Refuse to change what you believe. What you believe is the promise, so go back to the promise and reassure yourself. Get people of like minds, and ask them to agree with you.

CHAPTER 6

Stand on a Scripture

WHEN YOU BELIEVE in God to answer your prayers, you are expected to have a scripture you are standing on, not literally, but one that assures you of your request.

So search the scriptures and find one that talks about your needs. This is what helps to keep the communication line open with our Heavenly Father. Remember, God is a spirit and He communicates with us spirit to spirit.

Jesus said His words are spirit and life (John 6:63). When you find it, meditate on it day and night. Imagine you have your needs met. It will surprise you what benefits this brings (Joshua 1:8).

When you commit your life to Christ, you become a full-time student of His Word. How else would you get to know Him and grow? Heaven is now your destination, and you need to find out more about it even if you have a hundred years more to live on this side. What's more, you need to prepare in order to pass on to your children this new way of life (not religion).

What scriptures did we meditate on? They are all around in this book.

Scriptures are God breathed; they can kill, or they can bring life. Paul said the letter (scriptures) killeth (2 Corinthians 3:6). Jesus said, 'The words that I speak unto you, they are spirit, and they are life' (John 6:63).

> We have also, a more sure word of prophecy; whereunto ye do well that ye take heed, as unto a light that shinneth in a dark place, until the day dawn, and the day star arise in your hearts: knowing this first, that no prophecy of the scripture is of any private interpretation. For the prophecy came not in old times by the will of man: but holy men of God spake as they were moved by the Holy Ghost. (2 Peter 1:19-21)

> All scripture is given by inspiration of God and is profitable for doctrine, for reproof, for correction, for instruction in righteousness, that the man of God may be perfect, thoroughly furnished unto all good works. (2 Timothy 3:16-17)

First and foremost, what do I mean by meditation? It is the type of meditation Joshua, Paul, and the writer of Proverbs touched on (Joshua 1:8; 1 Timothy 4:15; Proverbs 4:20-21).

Let us look at how we as Christians meditate.

Meditation is thinking about the scripture, pondering over it, and turning it around in one's mind, like chewing to get every juice out of a piece of food. As you continue to do this, many things can happen – the Spirit of the Lord can take you all over or meet with you at the point of your need.

He can invite you to see Him in other scriptures, chapters, and verses, and bring you back to the particular scripture you chose to meditate on. You could meditate for a few minutes or hours; God will meet with you. God said if we draw near to Him, He will draw near to us. Spending time with Him in this way is amazing. It is rewarding, it builds faith, and it helps to see things from God's perspective. The scriptures will come alive. And whilst you are there before God for a specific purpose, He can use the opportunity to meet your other needs – how about that!

Let's read on about meditation.

Meditation

Ruminating or chewing on the Word like a cow chews cud, regurgitates, and then chews it again and again until the cow gets every bit of nutrient out of it. So is the act of meditating on the Word of God. If one can worry, then one has the skills to meditate, because worry is tantamount to ruminating on the negative about what will happen or not happen, what I should do or not do, what the negative consequences of my actions or no action are, and so on.

What are the practical steps we must take to meditate on the Word of God?

When we first begin to mutter a scripture or Word of God, it will feel as if we are being mechanical, like a robot. But as we give ourselves to it, it will take root and begin to have meaning to us because the Word of God has, inherent in itself, the ability to bring itself to pass. Did you get that? The Word of God is living, alive, and powerful. God likened it to fire and a hammer. The Bible says it is 'sharper than any two-edged sword'. It has the ability to wash our minds clean. The Bible also tells us that it is God breathed; in fact, it is with God, and it is God – that it became flesh. So as we are reading it as 'noun', it is being effective. And then as our faith develops, even during the process, we will actually begin to respond to what it is saying. And at that time, we will begin engaging with it as a 'verb', a doing scripture or word. A good illustration is this:

Take a word in the Bible such as 'hallelujah'. Mutter it over and over again; the word itself will begin to move mountains you cannot see (you will if sensitive enough), and you will hear of God manifesting on your behalf. This is the word acting as a noun. When you now begin to interact with it as a verb, doing what it says – such as actually praising God in singing praises, dancing, or being creative to glorify Him – you then get a whole lot more benefits.

In addition, the angels hearken to the words because they are commanded to. The devil and his demons also begin to feel the effect; they tremble, they are tormented, and they begin to scatter and flee. As they are resisted, they begin to grope in the dark as if blind; they are confounded and put into derision.

All this happens and more just because we meditate on His Word. Your brain changes for the better. Physiological, anatomical, biochemical changes and more take place to help your body heal.

> Sing o barren, thou that didst not bear; break forth into singing, and cry aloud, thou that didst not travail with child: for more are the children of the desolate than the children of the married wife, saith the Lord. (Isaiah 54:1)

As I meditated on these words, I could actually see myself with children. This is what is called Godly imagination. You must see in your mind's eye what you are believing in God for. It was like the scriptures were encouraging me to prepare for the arrival of my children – enlarge the place of my tent. We named our daughter Anna-Maria, but by the time I became pregnant, we had added another name – my sister's name, Janet. My sister played a major role in my husband and me coming to know the Lord (born-again), so I honoured her by naming my daughter Janet. However, Anna-Maria is still her womb name. I used to talk to my children when they were in my womb. I also sang to them.

The Word of God made a difference in my life; it became *rhema*, and it entered into every cell of my body and began to do a work of restoration.

Faith arose in me as I confessed the Word and pondered on it. I kept it in my heart day and night just as the scripture instructs us to do. Remember, we need to follow the Manufacturer's instructions.

The journey seemed long, but looking back, there needed to be a time of waiting. God actually told me in an audible voice that I would get the promise after my training. It happened during a period of crying and asking why the delay after so many prophecies. He spoke to me loud and clear. I have never since heard Him speak audibly to me. He does it more like an impression on my heart and sometimes by an inner hearing.

I must say He did startle me when I heard His audible voice. I was a baby Christian, and I might not have heard Him otherwise due to my spiritual immaturity.

Practical Application

Paul said to study to show you are an approved workman not ashamed (2 Timothy 2:15).

Do a bit of Bible study. Search for stories that are similar to yours and scriptures or promises that deal with your situation.

Write them out. These will become your medicine. Meditate on them day and night. You might even turn them into songs and sing them over and over again. Personalise the scriptures; they will hold more meaning to you.

The scriptures may be old, but it still retains the same power. The Bible tells us that God has made all spiritual blessings available to us. Jesus prayed a prayer, and He included everyone who will ever come to accept Him as Lord and Saviour – and that includes you and me (John 17:20-21). The scriptures are as powerful as when God said, 'Let there be light,' and there was light.

Therefore I will give thanks unto thee, O Lord, among the heathen, and I will sing praises unto thy name..

2Samuel 22:50

CHAPTER 7

Reprogramming

THE SCRIPTURES TELL us to renew our minds. How? By studying the Word of God. Research has shown that 87 per cent of the illnesses that man suffers is actually due to wrong thinking and that only 13 per cent is caused by genetic, neoplasm, metabolic, inflammatory, and degenerative conditions, to name a few (Caroline Leaf).

Dr Leaf, in her book *Who Switched Off My Brain?*, describes so brilliantly how this happens. She gives scripture upon scripture references and teaches us how to revert the damage done to our bodies. She encourages saturating your 'hippocampus' with the Word of God. I think it's a very good idea!

So how can the Word of God heal our bodies, including our minds? The Bible says, 'In the beginning was the Word and the Word was God.'

John 1 tells us the 'Word became flesh'. Jesus tells us that the word He speaks is spirit and life (John 6:63). Without even exploring this further, we know without a shadow of a doubt that the Word of God is potent.

Father God Himself tells us that His Word is not only like fire but it is also like a hammer (Jeremiah 23:29).

Moreover, in Hebrews the writer tells us that the Word of God is living, quick, powerful, and sharper than any two-edged sword, piercing even to the dividing of soul and spirit and of the joints and marrow, and is a discerner of the thoughts and intents of the heart (4:12).

Make no mistake; we need to interact with the Word of God, which means our mind actually needs to engage with the Word. Proverbs 4:20-22 tells us how.

> My son, attend to my words; incline thine ear unto my sayings.
> Let them not depart from thine eyes; keep them in the midst
> of thine heart. For they are life unto those that find them, and
> health to all their flesh.

It is an active process, an intermingling, an intercourse, and a serious business. Although the power of the Word in the right conditions produces instant results – hence a miracle – usually the people's heart is ready and waiting. There is usually an air of expectation, a longing, and a thirst; and in such situations, it is there and then that God shows Himself mighty. To maintain the miracle, it will require you to continue the fellowship with the Word of God.

Rest assured, God is not a man that He should lie. He will not change His mind.

> God is not a man, that he should lie, neither the son of man, that
> he should repent: hath He said, and shall He not do it? Or hath
> He spoken, and shall He not make it good? (Numbers 23:19)

The Bible says in Hebrews 11:11, 'By faith Sarah herself also received strength to conceive seed, and she bore a child when she was past the age, because she judged Him faithful who had promised.'

What meditation does for you is it makes the promise of God come alive in your heart and then you too can speak with the same level of confidence and faith that Sarah had.

The Word of God is alive and powerful. He created the universe, created you and me by His Word, and put His Word in our mouth.

> As for me, this is my covenant with them, saith the Lord; My Spirit that is upon thee, and my Words which I have put in thy mouth, shall not depart out of thy mouth, nor out of the mouth of thy seed, nor out of the mouth of thy seed's seed, saith the Lord, from henceforth and for ever. (Isaiah 59:21)

You might be saying, 'Oh, I have done that, and it doesn't work.' Well, this is where one needs to be truthful to oneself and ask the questions, 'Do I really believe? Is my faith strong enough?' These are questions we need to answer truthfully.

If you have not got the faith, then get it! How? you might say. By reading, listening, studying, and meditating on the promises of God. Listen to other people's testimonies and be encouraged. Faith comes by hearing; read Romans 10:17.

Revelation 12:11-we overcome by it. God is no respecter of persons.

Remember the wonderful Christian sister who sat on my bed and gave me her testimony on how she was barren but the Lord gave her a child? Well, she actually told me to meditate on Isaiah 54. It was one of the spiritual medicines I took, and it worked!

Testimonies have the ability to lift us up. It confirms the faithfulness of God, and it shows us that God is not a man that He should lie (Numbers 23:19).

The Bible also says in the epistle of Paul, 'Let God be true and every man a liar.'

It is never the Giver (God) that has the problem but us the receiver, says Andrew Wommack. We need to accept His promise (His Word) and wait for the manifestation. And in the meantime offer constant praises and thanksgiving unto God and worship Him, because faith pleases God. He said He honours His Word above His name (Psalm 138:2). What more assurance do we want?

Practical Application

Make a poster of these advantages and stick it where you can readily see it.

Meditation Advantages

1. Mind becomes clearer.
2. Emotions change.
3. Get solutions to problems.
4. Get answers to prayers.
5. Draw closer to God (He says He will draw close to you).
6. Faith building.
7. Confidence growing.
8. Self-esteem improves.
9. Anxiety reduces.
10. Blood pressure improves.
11. Joy rises.
12. Motivation increases.
13. Opens channel of communication with the Father.
14. Insomnia will disappear.

As for me, this is my covenant with them, saith the Lord; My
Spirit that is upon thee, and my Words which I have put in thy mouth, shall not depart out of thy mouth, nor out of the mouth of thy seed, nor out of the mouth of thy seed's seed, saith the Lord, from henceforth and for ever.

(Isaiah 59:21)

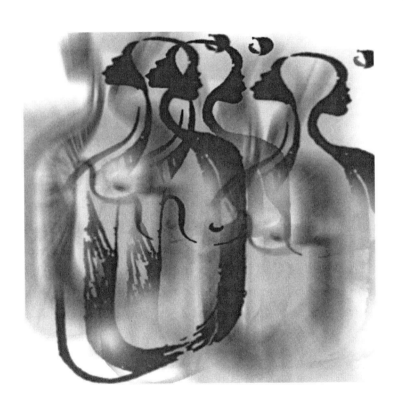

CHAPTER 8

The Parable of the Sower

JESUS DESCRIBES THE modus operandi (method of operation) of the Word. The Word of God is an incorruptible seed (1 Peter 1:23). When allowed to be engrafted into our mind, it will produce results (James 1:21). The Word that you sow shall become flesh. You will receive the desires you set out to get when you take the decision to sow the Word in your mind.

In Mark 4, Jesus explains the process of successfully sowing and reaping on good soil by being responsible, keeping watch, and not being careless.

Be determined that your heart (mind) will be a fertile ground to receive the seed of the Word and that you will nurture daily the ground and allow the seed to take root, grow, and eventually bear fruit (Jeremiah 4:3). Do not dig it out to see if it has started to grow. You may be disappointed and doubt why the seed must die first. This is what happens in the natural, if you remember your biology. If you focus on that, doubt might set in. Then the period of silence, when it seems nothing is happening to the seed (promise) that you've sown in your heart, is the season when the seed is dead and just beginning to germinate. The truth is, a lot is happening that is not visible to the natural eye. This is my interpretation of how I felt. David had the same experience when he asked God, 'Where is the word you promised?' So remain in faith, and do not waver. You do not need to know how the dead seed will later bring forth its fruit.

> And He said, so is the kingdom of God, as if a man should cast seed into the ground; and should sleep, and rise night and day, and the seed should spring and grow up, he knoweth not how. For the earth bringeth forth fruit of herself; first the blade, then the ear, after that the full corn in the ear. But when the fruit is brought forth, immediately he putteth in the sickle, because the harvest is come. (Mark 4:26-29)

The enemy will make an attempt to get you to dig out the planted seed, but you must resist the temptation. The Bible says resist the devil, and he will flee – run in terror (James 4:7). How do you keep nurturing your planted seed? By daily confessing the Word, the scriptures you are standing on, the scriptures that are your own *rhema*, the Word from God for your own particular situation. And no matter what, keep praising God.

The day will come when you will conceive. You will not see it physically at the moment of conception, but soon enough you will know, and then you will tell yourself that if God can keep the baby one day, He can surely bring the baby to full term. He said in Isaiah 66:9, will He bring to term and not deliver? Never!

The enemy disguises himself as an angel of light (Isaiah 66:9), so do not be deceived. He can speak through anyone, can appear on TV, radio, etc. Just remember that Abraham was fully persuaded that God who promised will bring His promise to pass.

God's law of sowing and reaping will stand for as long as this earth remains (Genesis 8:22). The Word is the seed, and it is incorruptible. Your heart and mind are the ground; when you confess the Word, you plant the

Word (seed) in your heart. Remain in meditation (Joshua 1:8), and allow the Word to take root, praising God in the meanwhile and taking steps of faith to show yourself that you actually believe you have your harvest. Like God, call those things that be not, as though they were, and the Holy Spirit will surely back up His promise if you do not doubt His ability to deliver (Romans 4:17).

Remember, when you plant a seed, it takes time to germinate and bring forth its plant. It doesn't happen overnight; however, things are happening underground that you cannot see. Not being able to see it does not mean that the process is not progressing. So it applies to the seed of God's Word in your heart. Resist digging it out, for example confessing wrongly. Say what you want.

Practical Application

Identify errors in your thinking, and realign your thinking with the Word of God.

Deal with any doubt in your mind, and remember that unbelief can exist alongside faith. James says if we are double-minded, we will never receive anything (James 1:8).

Our mind needs to be disciplined and should not to allow any garbage in. The world frequently speaks negative, but we can counter those negative words with the Word of God if we know the scriptures.

CHAPTER 9

The Waiting Time

But when the fullness of the time was come, God sent forth
His Son, made of a woman, made under the law, that we might
receive the adoption of sons. (Galatians 4:4-5)

WHAT IS THE purpose of waiting on God? I will discuss
this, taking my own situation into consideration and looking at the issue of
time from my own perspective. I was given some clue as to when I would
be ready for parenthood (spiritual insight), but in my distress one day, crying
to the Lord, I heard a voice loud and clear. It was not from a human being,
but the voice stopped me in my tracks, and I stopped crying instantly when
I heard the loud but non-threatening voice say, 'After your training!' I had
been working as a police doctor, waiting to go on training at the police
college. So I wondered, could it be that training? But I later understood that
it was spiritual training God was speaking to me about, the kind that would
prepare me for ministry.

Zechariah and Elizabeth were set aside to bring forth the forerunner of Jesus into the world, so Elizabeth had to be barren until the appointed time. God is never late. He is always on time. Lazarus was dead for four days; scientifically, he should have been smelling by the time Jesus got to him. Jesus deliberately took His time despite being given enough notice of Lazarus's death. For God, time is not an issue. In His own time He makes all things beautiful, and all we need to do is trust Him (Ecclesiastes 3:11).

You never know who you will be bringing to this earth, what assignment he or she will be given. God has an assignment for each one of us (Ephesians 2:10). Every barren woman brought forth a general, in the kingdom sense, with the exception of Michal, who became barren as a result of sin.

Looking back, I was not ready for children when I was living abroad. God had plans for me to accomplish a working life in the area of my speciality, which meant there were going to be lots of stressful times ahead, exams upon exams, moving from one post to the other, and many more situations that were not going to allow bringing up children. I knew He had called me into ministry in the area of service to the mentally ill, so I had to concentrate on my career. The Bible says that the gifts of God are good, and He added no sorrow. It is important that one is able to get on with life knowing that God has heard our prayers and will move at the right time. If one does not have that assurance, then more study of the Word to build faith is needed.

For God's time is always the best. In His own time He makes all things beautiful.

In Ecclesiastes, we are told there is a time for everything and God's time is always the best. If we are in tune with the Holy Spirit, time will not be an issue because we will constantly be reassured by the Word of God.

Abraham was a hundred years old, and Sarah ninety years old, and both well past the reproductive age. However, God had a purpose and a plan for them, and age was not going to get in the way. I was thirty-three years old when I first became pregnant. The children came one after the other. I remember a friend telling me not to wait another seven years before I had the next child after the first, and I laughed. A year later I fell pregnant with my second child, and he was six months old when I fell pregnant with my last child. I put in a request for my fallopian tubes to be tied after the third child. I became concerned that at this rate I would become a mother of a dozen! Isn't the Lord good? The Bible tells us that Jesus has come to give us life abundantly, and God's blessings are always mega. He opens the windows of Heaven and pours out blessing upon blessing with us having no room to put them. He is a 'much-too-much God', like Jesse Duplantis describes Him.

Jesus told us it is the Father's good pleasure to give us the Kingdom (Luke 12:32).

The Psalms tell us that God takes pleasure in our prosperity (Psalm 35:27).

God wants us to multiply, and He gives us children as a reward. We may have differing timings in bringing forth the next generation, but working closely with God will help us know the right timing.

One thing for sure among other things is that He provides great reassurance in His Word that everything will be all right. Let us look at Isaiah 64:4 and Isaiah 40:31.

> For since the beginning of the world men have not heard, nor perceived by the ear, neither hath the eye seen, O God, beside thee, what He had prepared for him that waiteth for Him. (Isaiah 64:4)

> But they that wait upon the Lord shall renew their strength; they shall mount up with wings as eagles; they shall run, and not be weary; and they shall walk, and not faint. (Isaiah 40:31)

Take time out and meditate on these scriptures, and see what they will do for you. Revisit the advantages of meditation mentioned earlier in this book, and be encouraged.

He has made everything beautiful in its time. (Ecclesiastes 3:11)

Practical Application

Do not become so preoccupied with having children that you neglect other things (e.g. career, education, dreams, goals, and aspirations).

Remember Ecclesiastes 3:1-8.

> To everything there is a season,
> A time for every purpose under heaven:
> A time to be born,
> A time to die,
> A time to plant,
> A time to pluck up that, which is planted,
> A time to kill,
> A time to heal,
> A time to break down,
> A time to build up,
> A time to weep,
> A time to laugh,
> A time to mourn,
> A time to dance.

And so the different times go on. Time is carved out of eternity – we must never forget – and eternity is in our hearts. God set eternity in our hearts.

God will be on time, and you need to be ready.

The Lord is the Alpha and the Omega, the Beginning and the End. He is ever present, He is eternal. To Him one day is like a thousand years, and a thousand years is like one day. God is never late; He is always on time. The Bible says He knows our frame. He knows that we are dust, yet it pleased Him to put His Spirit within us (eternity). How can we explain that? We cannot. We read in Ecclesiastes that there is a time for everything. It says in His own time He makes all things beautiful. God has a purpose for our lives. We are His workmanship created for good works (Ephesians 2:10). God brings Christians together in marriage to produce Godly offspring (Malachi 2:15). God has not forgotten you.

> For thou hast possessed my reins: thou hast covered me in my mother's womb. I will praise thee; for I am fearfully and wonderfully made: marvellous are thy works; and that my soul knoweth right well. My substance was not hid from thee, when I was made in secret, and curiously wrought in the lowest parts of the earth. Thine eyes did see my substance, yet being unperfect; and in thy book all my members were written, which in continuance were fashioned, when as yet there was none of them. How precious also are thy thoughts unto me, o God! How great is the sum of them! If I should count them, they are more in number than the sand; when I awake, I am still with thee. (Psalm 139:13-18)

If this does not convince you that your children are already in your loins (husband and wife), then I do not know what else will.

The Lord says He has a book and the book has details of your child. The very DNA that makes up your child is already pre-coded, and at the right time, not one second past, it shall be downloaded. Start praising God from today that He will make you a joyful mother/father of children. Worship Him, and dance before Him! And take practical steps of faith. Begin by preparing your child's room. Do something to prove to yourself that you believe.

Jesus said, 'Believe and you shall receive' (Mark 11:24).

God allowed the children of Israel to be taken into exile for seventy years. False prophets assured them that they would return home in a short while, but God informed them that they would stay out there for a very long time. So He advised them to marry, to build houses, to basically carry on with their lives, and to not become preoccupied with returning to home sweet home. God was moving according to His agenda and set time. When we ignore this fact, we can get ourselves into trouble. Father Abraham tried to move the goalpost; he took Sarah's advice and slept with her maidservant. Today the world continues to suffer the consequences.

During the waiting time, God continues to cater to our needs. He understands the anxieties we might have, and so the Bible tells us not to be anxious. Read Philippians 4:6.

Whilst we are waiting, our joy needs to be maintained, as the joy of the Lord is what gives us strength (Nehemiah 8:10). Also in Isaiah 40:31, we are told that those who wait on the Lord shall renew their strength, and such people will mount up with wings like eagles. It also says these people will run and not be weary, walk and not faint. This is a very powerful scripture worth meditating on when you have been waiting for some time. It will help you see things from the right perspective.

The children of Israel were in Egypt for four hundred years, but one day, they were out of Egypt, and Egypt was out of their lives forever.

Jesus' coming was proclaimed for years, and at the appointed time, He arrived (Isaiah 7:14; Zechariah 9:9; Micah 5:2).

We have to work with God every step of the way. He will never be late or too early, but He will always be on time. The vision may take long to come, but wait for it because it will surely come. Write the vision down. Wait for it (Habakkuk 2:3).

Practical Application

Read Ecclesiastes. Look at the timeline.

O lord, thou hast searched me, and known me.

Thou knowest my downsitting and mine uprising, thou understandest my thought afar off.

Thou compassest my path and my lying down, and art acquainted with all my ways.

 For there is not a word in my tongue, but, lo, O Lord, thou knowest it altogether

Psalm 139: 1-4

CHAPTER 10

TBC (Think, Believe, and Confess)

IT IS NEAR you; it is even in your mouth (Romans 10:8). In Proverbs, the writer says, 'As a man thinks so is he.' You are what you think. So the next step is for you to take everything you have been reading so far and realign your thinking with the Word of God. As you believe God's Word, begin to speak them into your life. The power is released when you speak God's promises into your life. All of Heaven backs you up, and the demons tremble because they know you now know God's truth and are indeed being set free. Hallelujah!

Jesus reminded us about the speaking of His Word. God told Moses to speak to the rock, but instead he struck it and forfeited the right to enter the promised land. We cannot afford to miss the promised land, the various promises that God has already assigned to our name. We need to claim them by calling them into being. This is the instruction God has laid down for us. Quantum physics shows us that living and nonliving things respond to words, thoughts, and intentions. How about that? God wants you to really get it. Now the ball is in your court, and in my court, we need to arm ourselves with a winning mentality and strike a victory.

Remember, life and death is in the power of the tongue. God's words are seeds, and they are incorruptible; our heart is the ground. If we take the Word of God and His promises and confess them (speak them), they will become engrafted in our minds; and if we are patient, they will yield a harvest. Many will testify this to be so. God gave us this gift along with everything else.

> For verily I say unto you, that whosoever shall say unto this mountain, be thou removed, and be thou cast into the sea; and shall not doubt in his heart, but shall believe that those things which he saith shall come to pass; he shall have whatsoever he saith. (Mark 11:23)

This is what Jesus said. He has made it so simple for us. This is how we get saved. We hear the Good News that Jesus died for us, we believe it with our hearts, and we then receive our salvation by confessing it.

> That if thou shalt confess with thy mouth the Lord Jesus, and shalt believe in thine heart that God hath raised Him from the dead, thou shalt be saved. For with the heart man believeth unto righteousness and with the mouth confession is made unto salvation. (Romans 10:9-10)

God said, 'Let us make man in our own image,' and He did. He said, 'Let there be light,' and light appeared. We too are encouraged also to speak His Word. Let us mimic our Father in Heaven; it pleases Him.

CONCLUSION

OUR PRAYER AND desire is that this book will be an encouragement to all those seeking God for the blessing of the fruit of the womb, irrespective of their circumstances, and to those who are believing God for the healing of their minds or any illness for that matter.

Search the scriptures; make the promise your own, the scripture that promises what you need, although no Word spoken by God is devoid of power. Meditate on His words day and night – i.e. ponder it, think about it, and turn it over in your mind until you get understanding. The Holy Spirit will interact with you in ways you can never imagine. Remember, meditation is not just reading; it is an active engagement that results in the practical ingestion of the medicinal potency of the Word. As you hear and absorb the Word of God, your brain and whole body will respond, your faith will increase, and before you know it, the harvest will turn up.

God bless you as you patiently wait for the promise.

God be praised in the name of Jesus.

END

Janet Browne, Teju olabode (cousin), Joshua Browne and
Jordan Browne at Lego land Windsor.

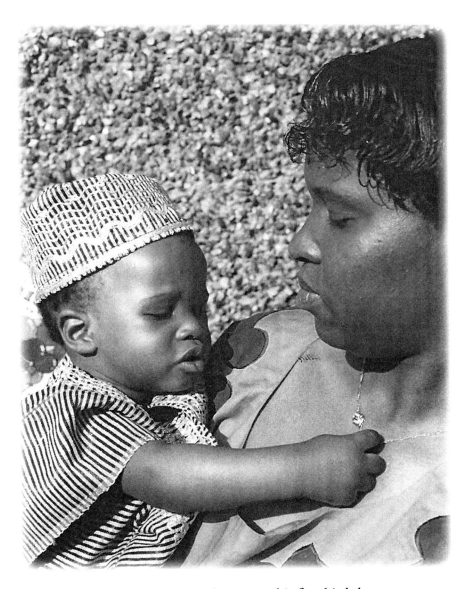
Joshua Browne and mum on his first birthday

Christina and Cornelius at Victoria Station London 1973

Christina and Cornelius 1994

Jordan Browne aged 5

Cornelius Browne 2009

Joshua Browne aged 7

Christina and Janet Browne 1995

Janet Browne aged 9

Lightning Source UK Ltd.
Milton Keynes UK
UKOW05n1630231114

242041UK00001B/24/P